# Through the EYES of a SATO

*Facing Fear & Finding Courage*

"INSPIRED BY TRUE EVENTS"
THE STORY OF

# Rico Suave

Copyright © 2018 by Gloria Silva

All rights reserved. No part of this publication may be reproduced, distributed, or transmitted in any form or by any means, including photocopying, recording, or other electronic or mechanical methods, without the prior written permission of the publisher, except in the case of brief quotations embodied in critical reviews and certain other noncommercial uses permitted by copyright law.

**For permission requests,**
**contact Gloria Silva**
1+ (973) 826-0309

**Published in 2018 by**
**Sato Fabulous, LLC**
P.O Box 752
Clifton, NJ 07015
www.satofabulous.com

IISBN-13: 978-1-7335592-0-1  (Sato Fabulous, LLC)
ISBN-10: 1-7335592-0-5

Printed and manufactured in the United States of America

"Sato" is a stray dog from Puerto Rico.

www.satofabulous.com

This is the amazing story of Rico, a courageous lil dog who was abandoned, forced to face a hurricane head on, and lived to tell his story.

One day, while taking my usual daily stroll through the sun-kissed streets of Humacao, Puerto Rico, I stumbled across my sato friends in the plaza, Tito and Diego from Salinas.

"Yo bro, wassup? What are you guys doing here? Woof!" I said.

Their tails were wagging fast, and they looked rather scared.

"Rico, don't you know? There's a hurricane coming straight towards us," said Tito in a rushed voice.

Diego kept looking around and said, "You know right now we are looking for a safe place on higher ground.

I heard the waves are taller than a house.

We can't swim through that."

My heart froze for a moment when I heard the news. I could not believe this was going to happen.

"Are you coming with us?"
Tito asked me.

I shook my head.
"I am sorry, I can't...
I have to alert my family.

Take care of yourselves,"
I barked and ran back home as
fast as my feet could take me.

"Woof, woof," I kept barking as I was getting closer. I wanted to warn mi familia of the danger, but as soon as I reached home, I noticed it was empty and boarded up.

Suddenly, I heard a familiar sound

*VROOOM, VROOOM.*

When I ran to the street,
I saw the car was driving away.

I tried to catch up to them.
I could see my hooman sister Anita
crying and pointing at me,
but they didn't stop.

I ran faster and faster until
I couldn't see them anymore.

"Ohh nooo! What am I going to do now? Woof! Where do I go?"

Then, I remembered my friends who said they were looking for higher ground.

Things quickly went from bad to worse!
Clouds rushed in, darkening the sky.

Wind, lightning, and thunder began
to roar like an angry monster.

*ROARRR!!!*

Swooshing rainfall caused flash flooding
and swept me away.

*What am I supposed to do?
Woof!* I wondered.

I tried to swim, but the current kept dragging me back. All sorts of debris kept churning towards me from every direction, making it impossible to see.

Until finally, I saw a fallen palm tree coming my way.

Hurricane Maria slammed Puerto Rico Sept. 20, 2017 as a Category 4 storm with 155 mph winds.

This is my chance, I said to myself and grabbed it's trunk with all my strength.

The tree floated for a while then drifted towards the side of a mountain.

I managed to jump out of the water
and crawl myself up to the
top of the mountain.

"Where am I? Woof! Where is everybody? Woof!" This place looked deserted.

All I could see was a muddy river with fallen trees, downed power lines, cars tipped over, as well as homes being washed away.

"It's getting darker and darker. What am I going to do?

I am hungry, thirsty, and scared. Owoooooooooo," I howled.

Suddenly, I heard footsteps. I looked up, and to my surprise it was Diego, Tito, and two other satos.

"You look terrible," Diego greeted me. "I thought you went back home? What happened?"

"I did go home," I responded, "but my family abandoned me and left me to face this terrible storm on my own."

"What? Then how did you get up to the Yunque?" said Tito.

"That's where I am, El Yunque! I always wanted to go to the rainforest but not like this," I exclaimed.

Rico, come over here I want you to meet Figaro and Chee-Kee.

They know these mountains like the bottom of their paws, said Tito.

"Okay guys, it's way too dark and dangerous for us to keep going.

We're gonna have to camp out here and start again in the morning," advised Diego.

The night was long and creepy.

The sound of crackling branches and raindrops kept me awake, while the others were sleeping.

Bright and early in the morning, we worked our way into the town in search of food and water.

There was nothing.

Rivers were filled with mud and garbage; everything was destroyed.

The storm destroyed hundreds of homes
and knocked out power leaving the entire island in a total blackout.

We wandered for miles, when suddenly I saw a light in the distance.

"Do you see that, guys? Something inside me says let's go there," I said.

They all nodded their heads and shouted, "YES."

As we continued our journey through the storm ravaged town, we began to see signs of life return.

We saw people cleaning, working together, and helping each other rebuild our enchanted island.

We saw a news reporter, a helicopter, and a man cooking and feeding hundreds of people.

He even threw us a few tasty bones.

The light became brighter and brighter as we got closer.

We started to jump for joy and ran because we were almost there.

Other satos started following us.

As we arrived, we found a woman
welcoming us with open arms
in front of a beautiful light house
filled with animals.

We were all fed and cared for.

Then I heard a sound.
Everybody, shhh shhh, listen.

Coqui, Coqui.

"Coqui" is a frog found only in Puerto Rico. It produces a distinct high pitched sound "ko-kee, ko-kee" especially at night.

We all looked at each other in amazement and chanted,

Puerto Rico will RISE!

WOOF!

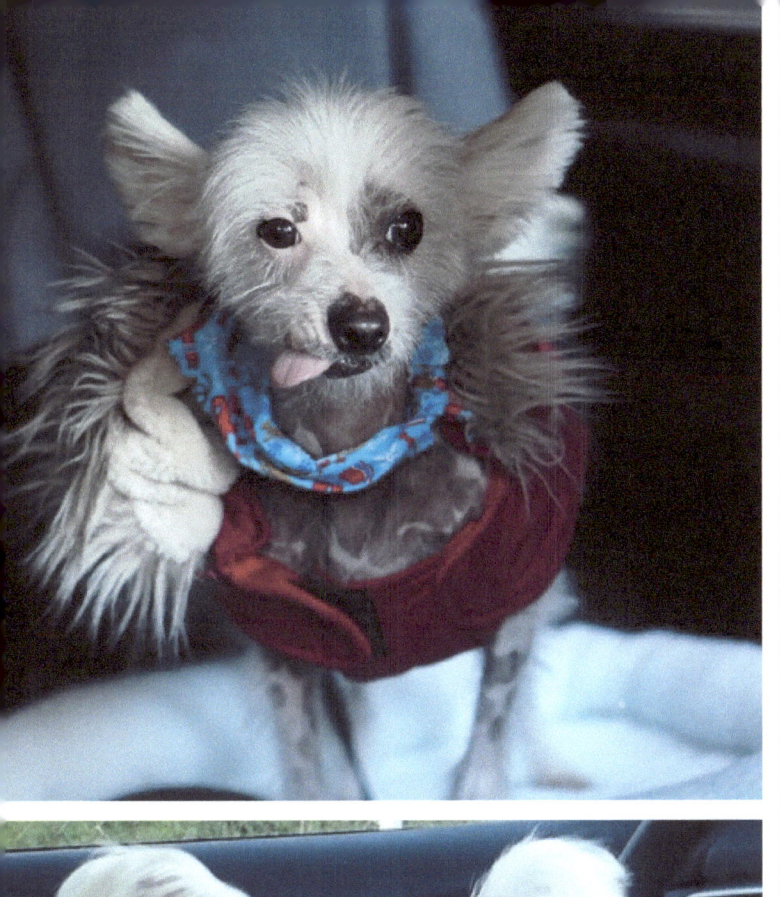

www.satofabulous.com

To my Superman husband, **Domingo Silva** for always believing in me and pushing me to the next level. Thanks for holding down the fort. Without you this book would've never happened. I love you now and FOREVER!

My childhood bestie **David Matos** for encouraging & inspiring me to write this book. Your insights influenced this book & stretched me. Thanks for walking this journey with me.

**Nancy Scott** & **Elizabeth Peluyera**, I will always remember and cherish the support you've given me. I value your friendship! My sister in law **Gladys Vazquez** for always being there.

**The Animal Lighthouse Rescue** for all of your amazing work rescuing and finding loving homes for the Satos. Especially blessing me with Rico Suave.

**David Begnaud**, Puerto Rico's Campeón. For your honest reporting, caring heart and not forgetting us. **Chef Jose Andres** and your team for your huge heart and determination to feed our Island.

**Governor Ricardo Rosello & First Lady Beatriz Rosello** for your dedication to the animals.

Most importantly to **God**, for surrounding me with LOVE everyday and NEVER leaving my side!

This book is dedicated to my grandson **Zakius Rodriguez**, remember to always DREAM BIG!

www.ingramcontent.com/pod-product-compliance
Lightning Source LLC
LaVergne TN
LVHW072126070426
835512LV00002B/21